THIS BOOK BELONGS TO:

_____

_____

Shop our other books at
www.sillyslothpress.com

For questions and customer service, email us at
support@sillyslothpress.com

RIDDLE 1

Hubert and Jared were fighting over a game. Hubert decided to settle the fight with a bet. He said to Jared, "If I write your exact weight on this piece of paper then you have to give me the game, but if I cannot, you get the game. Jared agreed, thinking no matter what Hubert writes he'll just say he weighs more or less. In the end Hubert gets the game. How?

RIDDLE 2

Look in my face and I am someone,

Look in my back and I am no one.

What am I?

RIDDLE 3

Why was the car sick?

RIDDLE 4

What invention allows you to see through walls?

RIDDLE 5

I can be cracked and I can be played. I can be told and I can be made. What am I?

RIDDLE 6

Two boys were playing darts. They played 7 games. Each boy won the same number of games. How is this possible?

RIDDLE 7

What starts with a *P*, ends with an *E* and has thousands of letters?

RIDDLE 8

Dolly rode into the city on Monday. Three days later she rode out on Monday. How is that possible?

RIDDLE 9

A rancher has 30 chickens, 12 goats, and 7 donkeys. If we call the donkeys goats, how many goats will the rancher have?

RIDDLE 10

What's the most slippery country in the world?

RIDDLE 11

What has ten letters and starts with gas?

RIDDLE 12

I am full of holes but can hold plenty of water. What am I?

RIDDLE 13

I have legs but cannot walk. I have a back and arms but reach not. What am I?

RIDDLE 14

What can honk without a horn?

RIDDLE 15

Where can you find buildings without people, oceans without water, and roads without cars?

RIDDLE 16

I bring famous people to your home every now and then. What am I?

RIDDLE 17

You throw away my outside, then you cook my inside. You eat my outside, then you throw away my inside. What am I?

RIDDLE 18

Louis and Iris were born to the same parents on the same day only 5 minutes apart, yet they are not twins. Why not?

RIDDLE 19

Which weighs more, a pound of feathers or a pound of stones?

RIDDLE 20

Multiply me by any number and the answer will always be the same. What am I?

RIDDLE 21

How do you get rid of the number one?

RIDDLE 22

What are moving left to right, right now?

RIDDLE 23

The month is July and you are on an island in the center of a lake. The lake is in a remote part of the country and there has never been a bridge connecting the island to the mainland. Every day a truck and cart give rides around the island. Confused as to how the truck had made it to the island, you ask around to find out that the truck was not transported by boat or by air. Nor was it constructed on the island. Can you figure out how the truck got there?

RIDDLE 24

What begins with T ends with *T* and is full of *T*?

RIDDLE 25

Why was the picture sent to jail?

RIDDLE 26

I take off my clothes when you put on your clothes. I put on my clothes when you take off your clothes. What am I?

RIDDLE 27

What do you call it when your parachute doesn't open?

RIDDLE 28

What goes up and down without moving?

RIDDLE 29

The chemist took two test tubes to experiment with. How many T's in that?

RIDDLE 30

What did the judge sentence the calendar thief to?

RIDDLE 31

One hundred feet facing the sky, but its back is on the ground. What is it?

RIDDLE 32

What building has the most stories?

RIDDLE 33

Everyone in the world needs it. They generously give it. But never take it. Then what is it?

RIDDLE 34

I have keys but cannot open doors. I allow you to enter and escape, but not to the outside. What am I?

RIDDLE 35

How can you throw a ball as hard as you can, to only have it come back to you, even if it doesn't bounce off anything?

RIDDLE 36

A clown was bragging at how long he can hold his breath under water. His record was 5 minutes and 34 seconds. A girl that was listening said, "I can stay under water for 12 minutes without any equipment!" The clown told her if she could do that, he'd give her $5,000. The girl succeeded and took home the money. How?

RIDDLE 37

A man leaves home and turns left three times only to return home again facing two men wearing masks. Who are the two men?

RIDDLE 38

I have no eyes, but you see me cry. I have no wings, but you see me fly. What am I?

RIDDLE 39

If two's company and three's a crowd, what are five and six?

RIDDLE 40

What resembles half a donut?

RIDDLE 41

I have a foot on each side and one in my center. What am I?

RIDDLE 42

What is more useful when it's broken?

RIDDLE 43

If an electric train is heading east, which direction is the smoke going?

RIDDLE 44

What does this mean? I RIGHT I

RIDDLE 45

What has no body and no nose?

RIDDLE 46

Why are ghosts bad at lying?

RIDDLE 47

I lose my head every morning but get it back at night. What am I?

RIDDLE 48

What is always late and never present now?

RIDDLE 49

What breaks when you say it?

RIDDLE 50

Using only addition, how do you add eight 8s and get the number 1,000?

RIDDLE 51

Why is it bad to iron a 4-leaf clover?

RIDDLE 52

I have no hands, no feet, no wings, no wheels, but I climb to the sky. What am I?

RIDDLE 53

What has a spine but no bones?

RIDDLE 54

I add four to ten and get two. The answer is correct, but how?

RIDDLE 55

I march but I am not in a band. I am known for my tuxedo, but I would be kicked out of a ballroom. What am I?

RIDDLE 56

I'm found in the paws of playful kittens. I'm found in scarves, socks, and mittens. What am I?

RIDDLE 57

Can you find the mitsake?

9988 8877 7766 6655

5544 4433 3322 2211

RIDDLE 58

They come out at night without being summoned. They are lost in the day without being taken. What are they?

RIDDLE 59

I pass before the sun but make no shadow. What am I?

RIDDLE 60

What word begins and ends with an E but only has one letter?

RIDDLE 61

Mrs. Pillow has 6 sons, and each son has a sister. How many children does Mrs. Pillow have total?

RIDDLE 62

Where do zombies go swimming?

RIDDLE 63

Choose a number between 1 and 10. Multiply it by 2, add 10, then divide it by 2. Now subtract the number that you have from the number you chose. What do you have?

RIDDLE 64

What do you get when you divide 50 by ½ and add 10?

RIDDLE 65

You'll find me in Mercury, Earth, Mars and Jupiter, but not in Venus or Neptune. What am I?

RIDDLE 66

I make a loud noise when I'm changing, and I grow larger and weigh less when I do. What am I?

RIDDLE 67

Why did the teacher wear sunglasses to school?

RIDDLE 68

How many seconds are there in a year?

RIDDLE 69

I have a neck but no head, yet I still wear a cap. What am I?

RIDDLE 70

You can hold me without using your hands or arms. What am I?

RIDDLE 71

How many 9's are there between 1 and 100?

RIDDLE 72

I can point in every direction but can't reach the destination by myself. What am I?

RIDDLE 73

When I point up it's bright, but when I point down it's dark. What am I?

RIDDLE 74

Ava only tells the truth on Mondays, Wednesdays and Fridays. One morning, she says, "Tomorrow I will tell the truth!" On which day did she say this?

RIDDLE 75

I am a five-letter word. I sound the same when you take away my first, last, and middle letter. What word am I?

RIDDLE 76

Four men were biking. It started raining, but only three got their hair wet. Why?

RIDDLE 77

A taxi driver is going down a one-way street in the opposite direction of traffic. A police officer sees him and waves. Why didn't the officer arrest him?

RIDDLE 78

Can you rearrange the letters, E O O W Y R N N D L O, to spell only one word?

RIDDLE 79

I don't bark or bite, but I still won't let you in the house. What am I?

RIDDLE 80

What type of room can people not enter?

RIDDLE 81

What goes up when rain comes down?

RIDDLE 82

During which month do people sleep the least?

RIDDLE 83

You have 5 children and need to get them all into a van. Scott and Mark are twins but they argue, so they can't sit together. Sasha and Ashley fight too, so they can't sit together. Jack argues with his sisters so he can only sit by his brothers. There are 5 seats side by side. How would you arrange the children, so that everyone is happy?

RIDDLE 84

I have a bed but never sleep. I have a mouth but never eat. I can run but never walk. What am I?

RIDDLE 85

What's the difference between a brand-new penny and a dirty old dime?

RIDDLE 86

If you are running in a race and you pass the person in second place, what place are you in?

RIDDLE 87

I'm hairy and soft from door to door. I'm like a cat that stays on the floor. What am I?

RIDDLE 88

What smells bad when it's alive but smells pleasant when dead?

RIDDLE 89

What kind of cheese is made in reverse?

RIDDLE 90

I can be short, or I can be long. I can be bought, or I can be grown. I can be painted, or I can be clear. What am I?

RIDDLE 91

A lion is on a 15ft chain but sees prey 16 feet away. How can the lion catch his prey?

RIDDLE 92

There were twenty chickens in a coop. All but twelve escaped. How many were left?

RIDDLE 93

What helps you get to room 313?

RIDDLE 94

No matter how much rain comes down on it, it won't get any wetter. What is it?

RIDDLE 95

What can you hold in your right hand, but not in your left?

RIDDLE 96

You're making breakfast and realize you have 6 bagels left. You know you will run out in one week, so you cut them in half. How many bagels do you have now?

RIDDLE 97

If it were two hours later, it would be half as long until midnight as it would be if it were an hour later. What time is it now?

RIDDLE 98

What has toes but no feet or legs?

RIDDLE 99

A boy said, "in 2 years I will be twice as old as I was 5 years ago." How old is he?

RIDDLE 100

What type of coat can you put on only when it is wet?

RIDDLE 101

If you toss a white hat into the Red Sea, what does it become?

RIDDLE 102

What can you add to a metal toolbox to make it lighter?

RIDDLE 103

It's Christmas Eve and Santa is ready to leave his workshop on the North Pole but lost his compass. Santa's elf says she will lead the way. What direction do they travel?

RIDDLE 104

How many birds can you fit into an empty cage?

RIDDLE 105

How many logs does it take to finish building a log cabin?

RIDDLE 106

You cast me away when you want to use me, but you take me back when you don't. What am I?

RIDDLE 107

When is a door not a door?

RIDDLE 108

I can wave but I never say hello. Use me when you're hot and I will cool you off. What am I?

RIDDLE 109

You go at red but stop at green. I have thick skin but can be cut deep. What am I?

RIDDLE 110

Five men attended church when it began to rain. Four men ran for shelter, but still got wet. The fifth man who stayed behind remained dry. How?

RIDDLE 111

I can be lost but not returned. What am I?

RIDDLE 112

I am a three-digit number. My second digit is four times bigger than the third digit. My first digit is 3 less than my second digit. What number am I?

RIDDLE 113

I never was but am always to be. I will always come, but you can't see me. What am I?

RIDDLE 114

There are 30 snakes in a room, and 28 rats. How many didn't?

RIDDLE 115

People buy me to eat, but never eat me. What am I?

RIDDLE 116

I am a seed with three letters in my name. Take away the last two, and I still sound the same. What am I?

RIDDLE 117

Which state is surrounded by the most water?

RIDDLE 118

You draw a circle. Without touching it, how do you make the circle bigger?

RIDDLE 119

You sing when I'm alive and clap your hands when I'm dead. What am I?

RIDDLE 120

What can you keep after giving it to someone?

RIDDLE 121

I no longer have eyes, but once I could see. Once I had thoughts, but now I'm empty. What am I?

RIDDLE 122

How can you make half of 12 equal to 7?

RIDDLE 123

What can you lose but still keep?

RIDDLE 124

What two things are impossible to eat at dinner time?

RIDDLE 125

Mary was driving home without her lights on.

The streets were not lit, and the moon was not glowing. Up ahead, a man was crossing the street. How did Mary see him?

RIDDLE 126

What type of bars won't keep an inmate in prison?

RIDDLE 127

If four women can bake four pies in four hours, how many pies can eight women bake in eight hours?

RIDDLE 128

What travels around the world but stays in one place?

RIDDLE 129

Before the discovery of Mount Everest, what was the tallest mountain in the world?

RIDDLE 130

Many hear me, yet no one sees me. I am born in air and I only speak when spoken to. What am I?

RIDDLE 131

What number do you get when you multiply all of the numbers on a telephone's number pad?

RIDDLE 132

The ages of a mother and daughter add up to 66. The mother's age is the daughter's age reversed. How old are they (there are 3 possible answers)?

RIDDLE 133

What do you call a cup that can't hold liquids?

RIDDLE 134

What is the end of the world?

RIDDLE 135

I am easy to get into, but tough to get out of. What am I?

RIDDLE 136

Which side of a chicken has the most feathers?

RIDDLE 137

What is the longest word in the dictionary?

RIDDLE 138

I am not old, but I stand in the cold. I am white and am quite a sight. Roll me up or knock me down. When I feel the sun, I start to run.

What am I?

RIDDLE 139

Everyone has me but no one can lose me. What am I?

RIDDLE 140

What goes round and round but never moves?

RIDDLE 141

I don't exist but I have a name. What am I?

RIDDLE 142

What can never be put in a saucepan?

RIDDLE 143

If you were born 6 years ago, how old would you be?

RIDDLE 144

At first I can be scary, but please don't retreat. I celebrate at night and by the end I am sweet. What am I?

RIDDLE 145

How can you leave a room with two legs and return with six legs?

RIDDLE 146

What kind of candy would a death row inmate want as his last meal?

RIDDLE 147

How many times can you divide the number 20 by 2?

RIDDLE 148

I can be played but I'm not a game.

I have keys but I don't open locks.

I have hammers but I'm not for tools.

I have pedals but I don't have wheels.

I can be tuned but I'm not a radio.

What am I?

RIDDLE 149

Take away my first letter, then take away my second letter. Then take away the rest of my letters, yet I remain the same. What am I?

RIDDLE 150

I go through cities and over hills, yet I never move. What am I?

RIDDLE 151

I am flat when you buy me and fat when you use me. I release my insides when something sharp touches me. What am I?

RIDDLE 152

What is at the end of a rainbow?

RIDDLE 153

What type of apple isn't an apple?

RIDDLE 154

Friday, Janice and Gus went out to eat. After their meal they paid the bill. If Janice and Gus did not pay, who did?

RIDDLE 155

I get sharper the more I'm used. What am I?

RIDDLE 156

What tastes better than it smells?

RIDDLE 157

I have every color, but no gold. What am I?

RIDDLE 158

I have been here since the beginning of time, but I am never more than a month old. What am I?

RIDDLE 159

Why can't a woman living in Alaska be buried in Texas?

RIDDLE 160

The more there is
the less you see.
Shine a light and
I will flee.
What am I?

RIDDLE 161

Why did the
thieves steal a
pack of cards?

RIDDLE 162

Where does
success come
before work?

RIDDLE 163

A cabin has 4 walls. Each of the walls faces south and a bear is circling the cabin. Can you figure out what color the bear is?

RIDDLE 164

How is the letter T like an island?

RIDDLE 165

I have eyes, but I cannot see. I stay in the dark until you need me. What am I?

RIDDLE 166

What has six faces and 21 eyes?

RIDDLE 167

Kyle is enrolled in four classes, Math, Science, History and English. He had an exam in every class and wanted to have some fun, so he did all his tests in Spanish. When he received his test results, only one teacher could understand his work. If none of Kyle's teachers spoke Spanish, which teacher was able to understand the test and how did they?

RIDDLE 168

What question can you ask at any moment of the day and get totally different answers, but all the answers could be true?

RIDDLE 169

Forward I am heavy, but backward I am not. What am I?

RIDDLE 170

What has four wheels and flies?

RIDDLE 171

The one who has it does not keep it. The one who keeps it may not want it. What is it?

RIDDLE 172

What has teeth but cannot eat?

RIDDLE 173

What has two hands, a round face, always runs, but stays in place?

RIDDLE 174

When is it bad luck to see a black cat?

RIDDLE 175

Take off my skin –
I won't cry, but you
might. What am I?

RIDDLE 176

I am a ball that can
be rolled but never
bounced or thrown.
What am I?

RIDDLE 177

Gaby is turning
21 this year, yet
she turned 20
yesterday. How can
this be possible?

RIDDLE 178

I get smaller every time you take a bath. What am I?

RIDDLE 179

What type of monkey can jump higher than a house?

RIDDLE 180

I have a bottom at my top. What am I?

RIDDLE 181

If you have me, you want to share me. If you share me, you haven't got me. What am I?

RIDDLE 182

What room do ghosts avoid?

RIDDLE 183

Water destroys me, but food nourishes me. What am I?

RIDDLE 184

I fill up a room, but I take up no space. What am I?

RIDDLE 185

The Berry family lives in a large, circular mansion. One day, Mr. Berry finds a chocolate stain on his new couch. He discovered that everyone at the house that morning ate chocolate pancakes. After reading the following excuses, figure out who smeared the chocolate.

Jenny Berry: "I was outside watering the plants."

Housekeeper: "I was dusting the corners of the house."

Chef: "I was preparing dinner for the evening."

Who is lying?

RIDDLE 186

If you have two coins which total 35 cents and one of the coins is not a dime, what are the two coins?

RIDDLE 187

I have many rings but no hands. I have many limbs but cannot walk.
What am I?

RIDDLE 188

People need me, but they always give me away.
What am I?

RIDDLE 189

What question can never be answered with a No?

RIDDLE 190

How do oceans say hello to each other?

RIDDLE 191

There is a beautiful clerk at the butcher shop. She is 5 feet 3 inches tall and wears size 7 shoes. She has a husband and 2 dogs. What does she weigh?

RIDDLE 192

What is always in front of you but can't be seen?

RIDDLE 193

I fly around all day but stay in one place. What am I?

RIDDLE 194

What gets wet while it's drying?

RIDDLE 195

Raul comes across three rooms. The first has sharp spikes on every surface, the second is engulfed in flames, and the third is full of jaguars that haven't eaten in 3 years. Which room is safest to enter?

RIDDLE 196

What do you set on a table to cut, but not to eat?

RIDDLE 197

Two mothers and two daughters went out for pizza. Everyone ate one slice, but only three were eaten total. How is this possible?

RIDDLE 198

Which letter of the alphabet holds water?

RIDDLE 199

A woman shoots her husband, then holds him underwater for 5 minutes. Next, she hangs him. Afterwards, they enjoy a lovely meal together. How is this possible?

RIDDLE 200

What word is right when pronounced wrong, but is wrong when pronounced right?

RIDDLE 201

Don bets Lilly $50 that he can predict the score of the soccer game before it starts. Lilly accepts, but loses the bet. Why did she lose the bet?

RIDDLE 202

What bank doesn't accept cash?

RIDDLE 203

What ship has two mates, but no captain?

RIDDLE 204

A woman dies of old age on her 25th birthday. How is this possible?

RIDDLE 205

Four chefs said that Evelyn was their sister. Evelyn said she had no sisters. Who is lying?

RIDDLE 206

You have 10 fig trees and need to plant them in 5 rows. Each row must have 4 trees. How do you accomplish this?

RIDDLE 207

I am a four-letter word. I can be written forward, backwards or upside down, and can still be read from left to right. What word am I?

RIDDLE 208

You can throw me off the tallest building and I won't break, but if you place me in the ocean I will. What am I?

RIDDLE 209

What can pierce one's ears without a hole?

RIDDLE 210

I am unseen but my presence is known. I will fade without a trace, but sometimes I linger. What am I?

RIDDLE 211

What is white when it is dirty and black when it is clean?

RIDDLE 212

What runs all around the yard but never moves?

RIDDLE 213

How many sides does a circle have?

RIDDLE 214

How many letters are in The Alphabet?

RIDDLE 215

Gaby purchased a $200,000 home but didn't have to pay a penny. How is this possible?

RIDDLE 216

Why did a musician group the letters A, E, F, H, I and K together and the letters B, C, D, G, J and O together?

RIDDLE 217

Why didn't the sun go to school?

RIDDLE 218

At times I am made of gold, but I cannot be bought or sold. What am I?

RIDDLE 219

How many plums grow on a tree?

RIDDLE 220

I am without bones and limbs, but if you keep me warm, I will soon walk away. What am I?

RIDDLE 221

How can you tell the difference between a jailer and a jeweler?

RIDDLE 222

Mr. Brown has two children. If the oldest child is a boy, what is the chance that the other child is also a boy?

RIDDLE 223

I am an eight-letter word. You can take my letters away one by one and I will still have meaning. Keep going until you have one letter left. What word am I?

RIDDLE 224

Each time you take a step you make one of me, but then you leave me behind. What am I?

RIDDLE 225

Which leprechaun wears the biggest hat?

RIDDLE 226

What has one eye open but cannot see?

RIDDLE 227

Imagine you're trapped in a room on fire. How do you escape?

RIDDLE 228

If a white house is white and a black house is black, what color is a green house?

RIDDLE 229

I am nonliving but I have a soul. I cannot taste but I have a tongue. What am I?

RIDDLE 230

What animal keeps the best time?

RIDDLE 231

Some months have 30 days, some months have 31 days. How many have 28?

RIDDLE 232

This belongs to you, but everyone else uses it. What is it?

RIDDLE 233

Why does heat move faster than the cold?

RIDDLE 234

I am an odd number. Take away a letter and I become even. What number am I?

RIDDLE 235

People beat and whip me, but they never see me cry. What am I?

RIDDLE 236

No matter how clever you are, there is one thing you will always overlook. What is it?

RIDDLE 237

On October 31st, a boy was rushed to the hospital emergency room. The ER doctor saw the boy and said, "I cannot operate on this boy. He is my son." But the doctor was not the boy's father. How could that be?

RIDDLE 238

A firefighter fell off a 25-foot ladder but was not injured. Why not?

RIDDLE 239

What four days of the week begin with the letter "T"?

RIDDLE 240

Mr. Orange sleeps in the orange house, Mr. Purple sleeps in the purple house, and Mr. Green sleeps in the green house? Who sleeps in the white house?

RIDDLE 241

What three letters can scare off a thief?

RIDDLE 242

If a wheel has 68 spokes, how many spaces are there between the spokes?

RIDDLE 243

What do you bury when it's alive and dig up when it's dead?

RIDDLE 244

What word contains 26 letters, but only has three syllables?

RIDDLE 245

What is as big as a hippo, but weighs nothing at all?

RIDDLE 246

What goes up but can't come down?

RIDDLE 247

What is the center of Gravity?

RIDDLE 248

What does a cat have that no other animal has?

RIDDLE 249

How do you spell candy in 2 letters?

RIDDLE 250

You can make me, but you can't see me. What am I?

RIDDLE 251

Why aren't human noses twelve inches long?

RIDDLE 252

What has one head, one foot, and four legs?

RIDDLE 253

I have two legs, but they only touch the ground when I'm not moving. What am I?

RIDDLE 254

I am a type of dress, yet you cannot wear me. What am I?

RIDDLE 255

I help you keep it together and I look like a tiny trombone. What am I?

RIDDLE 256

My pocket has something in it yet has nothing in it. How?

RIDDLE 257

There are two dogs in front of two other dogs. There are two dogs behind two other dogs.

There are two dogs besides two other dogs. How many dogs are there?

RIDDLE 258

What type of shoes does a plumber despise?

RIDDLE 259

I am an instrument through which sounds are made, but I cannot be played. What am I?

RIDDLE 260

What will the world never see again?

RIDDLE 261

Fire cannot burn me and water cannot drown me. What am I?

RIDDLE 262

I am the beginning of the end and the end of time and space. What am I?

RIDDLE 263

What word is spelled incorrectly in all dictionaries?

RIDDLE 264

Without me, you would lose your head. What am I?

RIDDLE 265

What does a shark eat with peanut butter?

RIDDLE 266

Who makes it, has no need of it.

Who buys it won't use it.

Who uses it, won't care.

What am I?

RIDDLE 267

You walk into a dark room with a match, a kerosene lamp, a candle and a torch. Which do you light first?

RIDDLE 268

What relation would your father's sister's sister-in-law be to you?

RIDDLE 269

How many peas are there in a pint?

RIDDLE 270

If your mom gave you three cupcakes and said to eat one every half-hour, how long would they last?

RIDDLE 271

How do spiders communicate?

RIDDLE 272

What do you name a fish without eyes?

RIDDLE 273

What has four eyes but cannot see?

RIDDLE 274

Turn me on my side and I am endless. Split me in half and I am nothing. What am I?

RIDDLE 275

You are a train conductor. Three men get on and seven men get off. Four women get on and one woman gets off. Another three kids get on and two kids get off. What color is the train conductor's hair?

RIDDLE 276

What five-letter word becomes shorter when you add two letters to it?

RIDDLE 277

What doesn't ask question but always needs an answer?

RIDDLE 278

One night, a chef, an artist, a cheese maker, and a dentist go to a diner. The server brings them a bill for five people. Who is the fifth person?

RIDDLE 279

I fly without wings. What am I?

RIDDLE 280

What kind of tree can you carry in your hand?

RIDDLE 281

You can throw me away, but I will always return. What am I?

RIDDLE 282

I am not alive, but I can die. What am I?

RIDDLE 283

What can be picked but not chosen?

RIDDLE 284

How is the moon like a dollar?

RIDDLE 285

You see a boat filled with people. It has not sunk but when you look again you don't see a single person on the boat. Why?

RIDDLE 286

What color is the wind?

RIDDLE 287

A man in a truck came across three doors. The first was made of rubies, the second was made of gold, and the third was made of the rarest wood. What door did he open first?

RIDDLE 288

What is tall when it is young and short when it is old?

RIDDLE 289

How is the number 8,549,176,320 unique?

RIDDLE 290

You live in a one-story house made entirely of limestone. What color would the stairs be?

RIDDLE 291

I begin all your sentences. What am I?

RIDDLE 292

What do you call
a bear without
bones?

RIDDLE 293

I reach for the
stars, but stand on
the ground.

Sometimes I leave,
but I am always
around.

What am I?

RIDDLE 294

Can you spell COW
in 13 letters?

RIDDLE 295

What gets bigger and bigger as you take more away from it?

RIDDLE 296

Angela's mother has 4 daughters – April, May, June. What is the fourth daughters name?

RIDDLE 297

Who makes a living driving their customers away?

RIDDLE 298

What jumps when it walks and sits when it stands?

RIDDLE 299

A boy is reading in his house when the power goes out. There are no flashlights or candles, yet he continues reading. How?

RIDDLE 300

I'm pinched by Grandmas and Aunts. What am I?

RIDDLE 301

What do you fill with empty hands?

RIDDLE 302

I am from a mine and am surrounded by wood. I will always be trapped and am used by almost everyone. What am I?

RIDDLE 303

I hold many memories but cannot think. What am I?

RIDDLE 304

Thirty people stand in an empty, circular room. Each person has full view of the entire room without turning their heads or bodies. Where can you place a peach so that all but one person can see it?

RIDDLE 305

If you put roast in a roaster, what do you put in toaster?

RIDDLE 306

I have thousands of needles but cannot sew. What am I?

RIDDLE 307

My days are numbered.
What am I?

RIDDLE 308

What gets broken if
it's not kept?

RIDDLE 309

A doctor and a pilot
are both in love with
the same woman,
Kara. The pilot had
to go on a long flight
and would not return
for a week. Before
he left, he gave Kara
7 apples. Why?

RIDDLE 310

Children love to play with me, but trees and wires could tangle me. I shake my tail as away I sail. What am I?

RIDDLE 311

I have two arms, but no fingers. I have a neck, but no head. At times I am clingy. What am I?

RIDDLE 312

If there are 5 horses, 3 dogs and one farmer, how many feet are there?

RIDDLE 313

If a rooster has black and white feathers, what type of chicks would hatch?

RIDDLE 314

What can clap without hands?

RIDDLE 315

I have a frame, but no photos. I have poles, but I cannot stand. What am I?

RIDDLE 316

I have a head
and tail but
no body.
What am I?

RIDDLE 317

What can you
serve but
not eat?

RIDDLE 318

What do you
call a nut with
a hole?

RIDDLE 319

I fall but I do not get hurt. I pour but I am not a spout. What am I?

RIDDLE 320

What is orange and sounds like a parrot?

ANSWERS

Answer 1: Hubert did exactly as he said he would and wrote "your exact weight" on the paper.

Answer 2: A mirror

Answer 3: It had gas.

Answer 4: A window

Answer 5: A joke

Answer 6: They weren't playing each other.

Answer 7: The Post Office

Answer 8: Monday is the name of Dolly's horse.

Answer 9: 12 goats. Calling the donkeys goats doesn't make them goats.

Answer 10: Greece

Answer 11: Automobile

Answer 12: A sponge

Answer 13: A chair

Answer 14: A goose

Answer 15: On a map

Answer 16: A television

Answer 17: Corn on the cob

Answer 18: They were two of triplets

Answer 19: Neither, they both weigh one pound!

Answer 20: Zero

Answer 21: Add the letter G and it's "gone"

Answer 22: Your eyes

Answer 23: It was driven over in winter when the lake was frozen.

Answer 24: A teapot

Answer 25: Because it was framed.

Answer 26: A clothes hanger

Answer 27: Jumping to a conclusion.

Answer 28: The temperature

Answer 29: There are 2 T's in the "that."

Answer 30: Twelve months

Answer 31: A centipede flipped over.

Answer 32: A library

Answer 33: Advice

Answer 34: A keyboard

Answer 35: Throw the ball straight up in the air.

Answer 36: The girl filled a glass of water and held it over her head for 12 minutes.

Answer 37: The catcher and umpire.

Answer 38: A cloud

Answer 39: Eleven

Answer 40: The other half

Answer 41: A yardstick

Answer 42: An egg

Answer 43: There is no smoke; it is an electric train.

Answer 44: Right between the eyes.

Answer 45: Nobody knows.

Answer 46: Because you can see right through them.

Answer 47: A pillow

Answer 48: Later

Answer 49: Silence

Answer 50: 888 + 88 + 8 + 8 + 8 = 1000.

Answer 51: You don't want to press your luck!

Answer 52: Smoke

Answer 53: A book

Answer 54: When it is 10am, add 4 hours to it and you get 2pm.

Answer 55: A penguin

Answer 56: Yarn

Answer 57: Mistake is spelled incorrectly.

Answer 58: Stars

Answer 59: The wind

Answer 60: Envelope

Answer 61: Mrs. Pillow has seven children. The six brothers share the same sister.

Answer 62: The Dead Sea

Answer 63: Do you have 5?

Answer 64: 110

Answer 65: The letter R

Answer 66: Popcorn

Answer 67: Because the students are bright.

Answer 68: 12. January 2nd, February 2nd, March 2nd, etc.

Answer 69: A bottle

Answer 70: Your breath

Answer 71: 20 (two 9's in 99)

Answer 72: Your finger

Answer 73: A light switch

Answer 74: Saturday

Answer 75: Empty

Answer 76: One was bald

Answer 77: He is walking

Answer 78: 'Only one word'

Answer 79: A lock

Answer 80: A mushroom

Answer 81: An umbrella

Answer 82: February (there are fewer nights in February).

Answer 83: Sasha, Scott, Jack, Mark, and then Ashley.

Answer 84: A river

Answer 85: 9 cents

Answer 86: Second place

Answer 87: Carpet

Answer 88: Bacon

Answer 89: Edam

Answer 90: Fingernails

Answer 91: The chain isn't attached to anything.

Answer 92: Twelve (one chicken is named Twelve).

Answer 93: An elevator

Answer 94: Water

Answer 95: Your left hand

Answer 96: 6 bagels

Answer 97: 9 PM.

Answer 98: Tomatoes

Answer 99: 12 years old

Answer 100: A coat of paint

Answer 101: Wet

Answer 102: Holes

Answer 103: South. If you're on the North Pole the only direction you can go is south.

Answer 104: One. After that it's not an empty cage anymore.

Answer 105: One brick

Answer 106: The anchor on a boat.

Answer 107: When it is a jar

Answer 108: A fan

Answer 109: Watermelon

Answer 110: The dry man was a body in a coffin and the other four were pall bearers.

Answer 111: Life

Answer 112: 141

Answer 113: Tomorrow

Answer 114: 10. Listen closely: 30 snakes, and twenty-eight rats. EIGHT and ATE sound the same. Thus, 20 snakes ATE rats. 30-20=10, so 10 snakes didn't eat any rats.

Answer 115: A plate

Answer 116: A pea

Answer 117: Hawaii

Answer 118: You draw a smaller circle next to it, so it becomes the larger circle.

Answer 119: A birthday candle.

Answer 120: Your word

Answer 121: A skull

Answer 122: Write 12 as a Roman numeral and draw a horizontal line through the middle.

Answer 123: Your mind

Answer 124: Breakfast and lunch

Answer 125: It was a bright and sunny day

Answer 126: Chocolate bars

Answer 127: 16 pies

Answer 128: A postage stamp

Answer 129: Mount Everest

Answer 130: An echo

Answer 131: Zero

Answer 132: 42 and 24. 51 and 15. 60 and 6.

Answer 133: A cupcake

Answer 134: The letter D

Answer 135: Trouble

Answer 136: The outside

Answer 137: Smiles, because there is a mile between each "s"

Answer 138: A snowman

Answer 139: A shadow

Answer 140: A washing machine

Answer 141: Nothing

Answer 142: Its lid

Answer 143: 6 years old

Answer 144: Halloween

Answer 145: Bring a chair back with you.

Answer 146: A life saver

Answer 147: Once, because after you divide it's not 20 anymore.

Answer 148: A piano

Answer 149: A postman

Answer 150: A road

Answer 151: A balloon

Answer 152: The letter W

Answer 153: Pineapple

Answer 154: Their friend, Friday

Answer 155: A brain

Answer 156: A tongue

Answer 157: A rainbow

Answer 158: The moon

Answer 159: Because she's still alive

Answer 160: Darkness

Answer 161: They heard there were 13 diamonds in it.

Answer 162: In the dictionary.

Answer 163: White. The cabin is at the North Pole, so the bear is white because it is a polar bear.

Answer 164: Both are in the middle of water.

Answer 165: A potato

Answer 166: A die (dice)

Answer 167: The Math teacher because numbers are the same in Spanish as they are in English.

Answer 168: "What time is it?"

Answer 169: Ton

Answer 170: A garbage truck

Answer 171: A gift

Answer 172: A comb

Answer 173: A clock

Answer 174: When you are a mouse.

Answer 175: An onion

Answer 176: An eyeball

Answer 177: Gaby's birthday is on December 31, the last day of the year. The current day was January 1st of the next year.

Answer 178: A bar of soap

Answer 179: Any, houses can't jump.

Answer 180: Your legs

Answer 181: A secret

Answer 182: The living room

Answer 183: A fire

Answer 184: Light

Answer 185: The housekeeper stained the couch. The house is circular and has no corners.

Answer 186: A quarter and a dime. One coin is not a dime, but the other one is.

Answer 187: A tree

Answer 188: Money

Answer 189: Are you alive?

Answer 190: They wave!

Answer 191: Meat

Answer 192: The future

Answer 193: A flag

Answer 194: A towel

Answer 195: The third. Jaguars that haven't eaten in 3 years are dead.

Answer 196: A deck of cards

Answer 197: They were a grandmother, mother, and daughter.

Answer 198: C

Answer 199: The woman was a photographer. She shot a picture of her husband, developed it, and hung it up to dry.

Answer 200: Wrong

Answer 201: Don predicted the score would be 0-0. The score of any soccer game is always 0-0 "before" it starts.

Answer 202: The riverbank

Answer 203: A relationship

Answer 204: She was born on February 29th.

Answer 205: No one. The chefs were Evelyn's brothers.

Answer 206: Plant the trees in the shape of a star.

Answer 207: NOON

Answer 208: A tissue

Answer 209: Noise

Answer 210: A fart

Answer 211: A blackboard

Answer 212: A fence

Answer 213: Two. The inside and the outside.

Answer 214: There are 11 letters in The Alphabet.

Answer 215: She didn't have to pay a penny, she had to pay $200,000.

Answer 216: The first group of letters is formed with straight lines while the second group has both straight and curved lines.

Answer 217: Because it already has a million degrees.

Answer 218: A heart

Answer 219: All plums grow on trees.

Answer 220: An egg

Answer 221: A jeweler sells watches. A jailer watches cells.

Answer 222: 50 percent

Answer 223: Starting is the 8-letter word. Starting, staring, string, sting, sing, sin, in, I.

Answer 224: A footprint

Answer 225: The one with the biggest head.

Answer 226: A needle

Answer 227: Stop imagining!

Answer 228: Clear. A greenhouse (for plants) is made of glass.

Answer 229: A shoe

Answer 230: A watchdog

Answer 231: They all do.

Answer 232: Your name

Answer 233: Everyone can catch a cold.

Answer 234: Seven

Answer 235: An egg

Answer 236: Your own nose.

Answer 237: The doctor was his mom.

Answer 238: He fell off the bottom step.

Answer 239: Tuesday, Thursday, today, and tomorrow.

Answer 240: The President

Answer 241: I C U

Answer 242: 68. The space that comes after the 68th spoke would be just before the first spoke.

Answer 243: A plant

Answer 244: Alphabet

Answer 245: The shadow of a hippo

Answer 246: Your age

Answer 247: The letter V

Answer 248: Kittens

Answer 249: C and Y, c(and)y

Answer 250: Noise

Answer 251: Because then they would be feet.

Answer 252: A bed

Answer 253: A wheelbarrow

Answer 254: An address

Answer 255: A paperclip

Answer 256: It has a hole in it.

Answer 257: Four dogs (in a square).

Answer 258: Clogs

Answer 259: Your voice

Answer 260: Yesterday

Answer 261: Ice

Answer 262: The letter E

Answer 263: Incorrectly

Answer 264: A neck

Answer 265: Jellyfish

Answer 266: A coffin

Answer 267: The match

Answer 268: This person would be your mother.

Answer 269: There is one P in a "pint."

Answer 270: One hour.

Answer 271: Through the worldwide web.

Answer 272: Fsh

Answer 273: Mississippi

Answer 274: The number 8. On its side, it looks like the symbol for infinity and when you cut it in half, it looks like two zeroes.

Answer 275: If your hair is brown, the answer is brown. If your hair is red, the answer is red etc.

Answer 276: Short

Answer 277: A telephone

Answer 278: One night can also mean one knight. The five people are: one knight, a chef, an artist, a cheese maker, and a dentist.

Answer 279: Time

Answer 280: A palm

Answer 281: A boomerang

Answer 282: A battery

Answer 283: A wedgie

Answer 284: Because it has four quarters.

Answer 285: Everyone on the boat was married.

Answer 286: Blew

Answer 287: The truck door

Answer 288: A candle

Answer 289: It's the only number having the names of all of its digits in alphabetical order.

Answer 290: What stairs? You live in a one-story house.

Answer 291: A capital letter

Answer 292: A gummy bear

Answer 293: A tree

Answer 294: SEE O DOUBLE YOU

Answer 295: A hole

Answer 296: Angela

Answer 297: Taxi drivers

Answer 298: A kangaroo

Answer 299: The boy is blind and is reading braille.

Answer 300: Cheeks

Answer 301: Gloves

Answer 302: Pencil lead

Answer 303: A picture frame

Answer 304: Place the peach on one person's head.

Answer 305: Bread

Answer 306: A cactus

Answer 307: A calendar

Answer 308: A promise

Answer 309: An apple a day keeps the doctor away!

Answer 310: A kite

Answer 311: A shirt

Answer 312: Two. Horses have hooves, dogs have paws, and only people have feet.

Answer 313: None. Rooster's don't lay eggs.

Answer 314: Thunder

Answer 315: Eyeglasses

Answer 316: A coin

Answer 317: A tennis ball

Answer 318: A donut

Answer 319: Rain

Answer 320: A carrot